Jesus my Boo

LOVE LETTER DEVOTIONALS

Tosha D.
JENKINS
PSALMIST

Cynthia
MARCANO
ENCOURAGER

Koren
UTLEY
LIFE COACH

FEEDING THOUSANDS PUBLISHING

URBAN
HOUSE
PUBLISHING

Feeding Thousands/Urban House Publishing

Publisher's Note: This is a work of non-fiction. Names and locations have been changed to protect the privacy of innocent and others. Locales and public names are sometimes used for atmospheric purposes. Any resemblance to actual people, living or dead, or businesses, companies, events, institutions, or locales is completely coincidental.

Book Layout ©2023 House of Cynthia Designs
Designed by StockVectors (Image #861976 at VectorStock.com)
First Edition 2022 – Jesus, My Boo: Love Letter Devotionals
Author: Cynthia Marcano, Tosha Jenkins, Koren Utley
Library of Congress Control Number: 2022922841
ISBN-13: 978-1-950913-18-3

Love Note

Heartbreak but also growing
pains to correct your vision
To realize **YOUR WORTH**
YOUR RELEVANCE
YOUR POWER

So my Beloved, please listen
We can create a *beautiful journey*
I just need your permission
To allow me to lead in your life
Would be your best decision
My love will wash over you
and soak you with wisdom

Let's link in truth and flow in divine rhythm
Let go of troubles, give it all to me
I'll take it all and flood your being with peace
Create an *overflow of love* you will have for me

You are a **TREASURE TO BE TREASURED** for eternity
Heartbeat skips, you may lose your breath
As each worry disappears until there's none left

What I will do for you, no one else can
Unconditional love from,
I AM THAT I AM

by Tosha Jenkins

DEAR FUTURE ME,

I'm experiencing a season of heartbreak. Someone we love is gone from our lives. I would have never imagined that I could feel such deep pain. Heartbreak is more than just a phrase. It is agonizingly accurate because I promise you, I feel actual physical pain. I place my hand where my heart is and try to console the constant ache residing there. I am broken in heart, mind, & spirit.

The tears I cry do little to bring me comfort, but I cannot help but let them fall freely in an effort to find an end to this pain. Perhaps, I have not shed a sufficient amount to satisfy God. My heartache is profoundly hurt enough to produce more, of that I am sure. I'm unable to keep from soaking my pillow every night, despite me begging God to take away it all away. I would gladly give up having emotions if He would just take this pain from me.

Yet, if I'm honest, what my heart truly wants is the love of the one who left me. Their love is the cure to what ails me. That we have more happy days ahead.

I feel lost & lonely. Unloved & abandoned. Am I not enough? Is God punishing me? Future me, when will this pain end? Does my heart mend? Will I ever be happy again?

Please write back soon. I am desperate.

Hurting,
Your Heartbroken Self

DEAR PAST ME,

I remember our pain so vividly. The grief we felt was all-consuming, affecting nearly every other part of our lives. It was indeed a difficult season of heartbreak.

You asked several questions that I am eager to answer, but first I have to tell you that while I am so sorry that we had to endure that season in our lives, I wouldn't change it. I know that probably surprises and even frightens you, but please let me explain a little further.

First, I don't mean that I am glad we suffered. That's not what I mean at all. What I really mean is what was produced from that pain is something that I have come to cherish and not something I would give up.

You see while we were suffering and crying out to God, He heard every plea and collected every tear and although we didn't know it, He had a plan to make it all ok. He used what the enemy meant to destroy us, instead to mold and strengthen us. Thinking back on that misery, I know how close we were to jumping off the ledge of life & sanity, our misery being watered with the poison that the enemy rained down on us minute after minute. Oh, Past Me, we were wounded and barely alive inside. Yet, what we saw as death, God saw as an opportunity for resurrection.

Past Me, you ARE more than enough. God made you more than enough. You have to believe that about yourself. And because He is loving, He will always place others in your path that will validate His love for you, reminding you that you are enough. I am very happy to report that God does send us a true and dear friend. A Godly woman that feeds our spirit and we in return we feed hers. She is absolutely amazing. We have indeed been blessed.

God loves us and while we have fallen short, as all man does, He sent His son to take on our iniquities. He heard your plea for forgiveness and has forgiven you. It's time to let that go. Stop punishing yourself and walking in shame that has been discarded. God remembers it no more.

Your pain was not in vain. It becomes a necessary part of your journey. It is because you felt so heartbroken that you learn to rely on Christ to heal you. You study scripture and pray daily in search of hope and comfort. You surrender it all to Him. God doesn't take your pain away, Past Me. However, He teaches you to give it all to Him so that He can carry it. He teaches you to rely on Him and trust Him with your future. He teaches you to let go. He teaches you to love yourself because you are beautiful.

Past Me, you become a Heartbreak Survivor, then a Thriver, and eventually a Riser. You begin a ministry that is dedicated to helping others suffering heartbreak. Your journey was more than just getting over heartbreak. It was God molding you and giving you the tools needed to do more than just be happy again one day. His plans are bigger for us than we can fathom.

And lastly, yes, Past Me, you are beautifully mended.

Hang on! God loves you, as do I. His love never fails.

With Profound Love,
Your Future Self

I say this because I know what I have planned for you," says the Lord. "I have good plans for you. I don't plan to hurt you. I plan to give you hope and a good future.
Jeremiah 29:11 ICB

love note...

BELOVED, I VOW TO LOVE YOU AS MY BRIDE, DAUGHTER, & FRIEND...

Love never gives up.
Love cares more for others than for self.
Love doesn't want what it doesn't have.
Love doesn't strut,
Doesn't have a swelled head,
Doesn't force itself on others,
Isn't always "me first,"
Doesn't fly off the handle,
Doesn't keep score of the sins of others,
Doesn't revel when others grovel,
Takes pleasure in the flowering of truth,
Puts up with anything,
Trusts God always,
Always looks for the best,
Never looks back,
But keeps going to the end.
Love never dies.

1 Corinthians 13:4-8 MSG

His Beloved Bride

A TESTIMONY BY CYNTHIA MARCANO

I crashed against the table and watched as the man who'd thrown me against it, turned away seething in anger. My back ached from the impact. My face burned from both, the hostility I felt welling up within me and from the residual pain of his forceful grab. His massive hands squeezed my face tightly, shaking me senseless before mushing me. It was humiliating. It was scary. It was time to go.

For two years I battled the indecision to stay or to go. I was a Christian woman. One with a flourishing ministry dedicated to marriage restoration. For over thirteen years I had been fighting for my marriage. After my husband cheated two months after our wedding, I fought. After he filed for divorce five years later, I fought. After he cheated the third time, I fought. I fought and each time we reconciled. I encouraged others to fight. I wrote books about not giving up on marriage.

Until two years ago when the idea that I was fighting for someone who was fighting against me, not with me, not for me, but against me, crept into my heart. And then I fought that. God could change anyone. He could change my husband. Had he not changed me? Yet, my husband hadn't changed since giving his life to God ten years earlier. Hadn't the last infidelity been a clear indication of such? Hadn't the emotional and mental abuse year after year been evidence of that? Yet, divorce was not an option. I contemplated downing a bottle of Oxycodone, the idea a less frightening option than divorce, just to escape what had become a wall-less prison. A truth I admitted to my husband once, to which he only responded that I was an idiot before walking out of the bedroom.

I walked away from the table that had crashed into the wall, in the similar way I had crashed into it, abandoning the groceries I had been putting away, and retreated to my bedroom, stupefied at what had just occurred. Chaos erupted so quickly I could hardly wrap my mind around it. Sitting atop my bed, memories came down on me like an avalanche.

I recalled the time my husband made me wait outside on the curb of his job, like a dog that wasn't allowed admittance, while he went inside to introduce my then toddler daughter to his co-workers. I remembered when we were returning from seeing his gravely ill father and he upgraded his flight to first class and booked me in coach. My heart sickened thinking of when I laid in the hospital bed after having my youngest child, and he was sitting beside me texting another woman. Tears rolled down my face remembering being married for just two months and waking up to his phone ringing only to answer and it was a woman he had met online. The tears increased remembering I didn't leave him that very day because I found out I was pregnant hours later.

With poignant clarity, the venomous words he spewed at me, buzzed in my ears. Lazy because I spent a large part of the day breastfeeding my baby. Unmotivated because we decided as a couple that I would be a stay-at-home mom. Disgusting because three children made it hard to keep the house pristine at all times. Disloyal to him because I loved my family and wanted to spend time with them. Disobedient because I dared to follow a dream that didn't involve him. Irresponsible because I went to the gas station that was three cents more expensive per gallon than the one further down the road. Inconsiderate of his money because I wanted to purchase Christmas decorations with the kids.

Yet louder than his words of disdain, were my own of self-loathing. Naïve. Stupid. Foolish. My thoughts had become traitorous, and I began to wonder when I had aligned myself with my husband's way of thinking. When had I begun to emotionally and mentally abuse myself? It didn't take long to figure out. While my husband had indeed heaped enough upon me to

11

wound my emotional and mental state severely, my own actions nearly drove me off the cliff.

I hadn't realized how much I longed for true companionship until I was past the point of emotional attachment to a male friend who had eased into my life gently and unexpectedly. There was no intent of wrongdoing at the inception of our acquaintance, but nevertheless it became so and the sin of attachment to a man who wasn't my husband was shackled to me. And I knew it was wrong. I prayed for God to somehow let me be white as snow in His eyes, while keeping the friend who had become so near and dear to me. Why was it so wrong to have someone who listened and didn't judge? One who motivated instead of ridiculing? A man who loved the Lord and was always eager to share a Word with me? A person who was equally attached? Yes. It was emphatically wrong and yet I did not know how to walk away. Oh, I tried. Many times. We both had. But somehow, we always ended up back at being friends, until God removed what I couldn't.

Since giving my life to Christ over a decade ago, I had lived a mostly squeaky-clean life, at least in my own estimation. I prided myself on being a devoted and Godly wife as well as a humble and giving servant. I had served in ministry and taught bible study. I had been a loyal wife, always being the first (and only) to forgive quickly, aiming to please constantly. Daily, I poured into others in my own ministry. I authored books that encouraged others and developed a following that had brought me a small measure of notoriety.

But that all meant nothing. I was a sinner and would always be a sinner. My actions proved that to be true. I was no different than my husband and if since that was true to me, how could I possibly think I had a right to escape my prison? I deserved every ounce of abuse hurled upon me. It was my cross to carry. So, I carried that cross. I said nothing when we moved and my husband did not include me on the lease agreement, making me essentially homeless. I carried the cross and said nothing when he lied and told people I had spent the night with my friend resulting in a physical affair, a complete falsehood. I said nothing when he neither came to the hospital nor helped care for me after major surgery. I remained quiet when he told anyone who would listen than I was an adulteress.

While I said nothing, I began to look out my prison window and dared hope that life had more to offer, even within my prison.

My newfound hope was a strangely exciting event in my life. Once I dared lay down a steppingstone of faith and hope, other stones soon followed, and before I knew it, a path had begun to form at my feet. One small hope of surviving another day, led to many other things to hope for. First and foremost, was finding a job after being a stay-at-home mom for fourteen years. Freedom required funds of which I had absolutely zero. My husband's income was just that – his income.

I prayed and heard God whisper in my ear the name of the employer that I worked for before I got married and moved away. Within two days of applying, I received a call for an interview. When I arrived at the interview a week later, I was greeted by someone I had worked with many years ago, who turned out to be the director of the department. She hugged me and told me that it wasn't an interview at all, as I had already had the job. To God be the glory! Not only was I blessed with a new job right away, but I had also learned that the department I would be working in had just moved to a facility three blocks from my apartment the month before, making my commute easy. Won't He do it!

My husband was not excited about my new opportunity and how quickly I had landed a job. In his controlling way, he squashed my joy by allotting my entire future paycheck to bills, leaving me twenty dollars per pay period to myself. I didn't complain and instead decided to open a savings account and save every extra penny that I earned. The earnings from my book sales were meager at best, but I saved that too. For the first time in nearly fifteen years, I felt like I was doing something that was just for me and didn't need anyone's permission. He called it selfishness, but I couldn't or wouldn't care.

There are times in our lives that alter the course of our future. Sometimes they are so subtle we can't pinpoint that exact moment. Other times, they are larger than life and we remember them vividly. And then there are times, it's only in retrospect that we can see where the paths of our lives changed. Opening a savings account for myself was the equivalent of a chisel and hammer pounding into concrete – eventually a crack will form. While my marriage's foundation had never been stable due to the infidelity from the beginning, it took many years before it began to crumble to the point of no repair. For years, I had been patching the cracks. Now I found myself letting it crumble along with the cracks I had hammered into it.

As I sat on my bed and cried, I made the decision to finally let go. Our last-ditch effort at marriage counseling with our Pastors had been one of the worst experiences of my life as he sat there and lied, playing victim. Talking to him had changed nothing. Asking God to change someone was fruitless. We have our own free will. God was more interested in me wanting to change myself. So, I did. I made the decision to not be a punching bag. I decided to continue paving my path and trusting God to lay the stones before me. I decided that what others would think or believe was not my concern.

Most importantly I decided to continue to let God guide me without fear. No longer would I patch up the cracks. No longer would I allow the enemy to guilt me into staying. God hated divorce, but He did not hate me. That finally sank in. God knew my heart and how hard I had tried. He would be my husband, just as I was His bride.

Two months later I moved into my own apartment. It was small and bare, but it had a peace that I wouldn't trade for all of the furniture in the world. After several months of prayer and guidance, I finally filed for divorce. It was one of the most difficult decisions of my life, but a necessary one.

Healing from an emotionally abusive relationship takes time. Learning to love yourself, trust others, set boundaries and believe you deserve better than abuse is difficult but not impossible. Every day is a choice to believe I am worthy.

God says I am beautiful in every way. Song of Songs 4:7.
He says I am fearfully & wonderfully made Psalm 139:14.
He says I am His beloved. Isaiah 49:16.
He says I am His Bride. Revelation 19:7-8.

I have used that pain to begin a new ministry dedicated to helping the heartbroken survive abuse, divorce, betrayal, rejection, abandonment or whatever circumstance has brought them pain. My path has led me through both valleys and mountaintops, but my Heavenly Husband has been with me through it all, ushering me into freedom and unfathomable peace.

love note...

BELOVED, WHEN YOU ARE HEARTBROKEN, KNOW THAT I AM JEHOVAH-SHALOM, THE GOD OF PEACE AND COMFORT ...

Jesus said, "Come to Me, all you who labor and are heavy-laden and overburdened, and I will cause you to rest. [I will [a]ease and relieve and [b]refresh [c]your souls.]
Matthew 11:28 AMPC

Jesus said, "Don't let your hearts be troubled. Trust in God. And trust in me."
John 14:1 ICB

Jesus said to her, "I am the one who brings people back to life, and I am life itself. Those who believe in me will live even if they die.
John 11:25 GW

I have said these things to you, that in me you may have peace. In the world you will have tribulation. But take heart; I have overcome the world."
John 16:33 ESV

HE LEFT ME, HE FOUND ME

My love left me. It wasn't the first time. My heart stupidly yearns for him. My unfeeling brain tells me to get over it. The push and pull within, rips me in half just like a cheesy paper heart torn in two. Yet, no other image I can conjure up is more accurate to describe the ache I feel inside. The emptiness. The loneliness.

How can a person invoke such joy and yet such agony? How can my heart still long for the one who broke it? Why can't I move on as easily as he did? Why did he move on? Am I not worthy of lasting love? We laughed. We loved. We cried. I gave him everything. I still want to give him everything. I want to add his name to mine in the love equation that equals forever. I want him to call to tell me he made a huge mistake. That he is coming back. That he never meant to hurt me. I want him to end this pain.

Yet, I've circled Broken Heart Boulevard too many times and I can't travel down it again. I need to take the next exit off this road. God is telling me to take the upcoming ramp to healing. He is ready to ride shotgun, strapped in for the long haul. There is no one else I'd rather take this road trip with. He knows the way to the Promised Land. I trust His navigational skills.

He promises to not just get me to the land that flows with wholeness and healing, but that He will be my Everlasting Love. That He will never leave me. He won't make me cry. That many days of love and laughter are yet to come. That to Him, I am worth dying for. I am worth dying for. Me. Yes, me. The thought makes my broken heart skip a beat. I am loved.

Right now, my heart still longs for the one who left, but the One that is here, is more than enough. He is fixing my broken places and filling empty spaces. He wants to be my all. He wants to give

ME everything. What a concept. My love left me. It wasn't the first time, but it will be the last. Whether God chooses to restore my love to me or not, I will never be alone again because I choose my Everlasting Love and He will love me forever and ever.

I have loved you, O my people, with an everlasting love;
with loving-kindness I have drawn you to me.
Jeremiah 31:3 TLB

AsKoren

Dear Koren,

I've been divorced for many years now and after such a heartbreaking ordeal, I decided to live the rest of my life as God's bride alone. However, for several months now, I find myself contemplating getting married again one day. I'm struggling with the idea of even entering the dating life at my age and if God would bless a second marriage. Any advice how to navigate would be appreciated.

Dear Reader:

Congratulations on dedicating your life to the Lord. I understand your concerns about dating and remarrying. Starting over isn't always easy, but it can be the start of a beautiful beginning with someone you can build, grow, and dream with. Divorce is unfortunate, but it's not a death sentence. God loves you so much that He's willing to give you another chance at loving, and building a life with a new partner. God honors marriage and teaches us how to build a covenant with one another. With an open heart and mind, I believe you will be fine. Decide what you want and be clear about it. If you continue to seek the Lord, you will find direction and fulfillment.

Koren,

Bold and Brilliant, Founder
Self-Development Coach

Nobody But You

Things in my life were changing
I was changing

Doing the inner work sometimes hurt
But chasing after You made it worth it

You are perfect
Yet my imperfections,
lessons, and experiences
were needed
I refused to feel defeated
Especially, when I have
You in my life,
in my corner,
and by my side

There were days, I cried and cried
Knowing You are close to the broken-hearted,
started a comfort that cushioned the pains and weariness

Dramatic changes,
turning to new pages
My love for You rages
as I reach different stages
in this journey

Tears of pain and anguish now tears of joy and peace
You lit a fire within, set ablaze to light the way

Depending on only You
And believing I am safe in Your Hands has changed my life

I include You in all that I do
And when the blessings come
I KNOW IT WAS NOBODY BUT YOU

by Tosha Jenkins

LET GO, LET GOD

I am currently on a season-changing journey in my life to release people, places, and things. It isn't as easy as I wish it was, but necessary all the same. Today makes day thirteen of letting go and moving forward. Yes, I am counting the days because each day that I move forward, is a victory for me. I count each victorious day and give God praise for helping me through it.

You see, I am not leaving behind people, places, and things that I despise or that I don't care for. That would not be a journey. That would be easy and not worth mentioning. I have a love, liking, respect for all that I am letting go. Letting go has taken a toll on my heart, mind, and soul.

You are probably asking why I am letting go of what obviously has a hold of my heart. My answer is simple. God has called me to do so. For too long I have gone back and forth fighting this journey. At God's first urging, I doubted He told me to let go and didn't. At His second calling, He removed what I couldn't because I had been disobedient. It took me so long to see that, always blaming the enemy or my other circumstances, always finding a reason to hang on rather looking inward at my own folly.

A really good friend of mine made it clear that interfering with what God was setting in motion was dangerous and that it was time to let go instead of watering the fig trees in my life that refused to produce fruit. My heart is stubborn and while I wanted to be obedient to God and heed the counsel of my friend, it wasn't so easy to just turn off what I wanted. It took accepting the hard truth that my flesh was ruling my life and I could no longer allow that.

By flesh, I am not referring to anything sexual, but instead, wanting what I wanted and what I thought was best for my emotions. I didn't want to hurt. I didn't want to go through change. I didn't want to start a new chapter in my life. I didn't want to release things that kept me rooted to the past. Like a smack to my face, I realized I was choosing what I WANTED. I was choosing carnality over God. That was the wake-up call I needed.

So here I am. Day thirteen of letting go and moving forward. Day thirteen of choosing God.

I downloaded this nifty app on my phone and each day I journal thoughts to keep me motivated and keep track of how I am reaching toward the prize of walking the journey God has planned for my life. Whenever I am tempted to go back to my past, I take a look at my journey thus far, how far I've come already, and I remember that I am right where I am supposed to be. I see God in my walk, and I hunger to add many more victorious days to moving forward in my life. I want to reach the milestones that God has placed in my heart. I am moved to be changed, renewed, restored, or whatever else God is calling me to.

Are you struggling to move forward in your life? Is your heart stuck, in need of release? I understand more than you know. I also know that until you take the first step, the hardest step, you will stay stuck. Soul ties, comfortable places, and attachment to physical things are not easy to let go of but are not worth missing God's plan for your life. Make up your mind to love both God and yourself more. Make up your mind to reach for the prize of a healed and whole heart, mind, and soul.

I press toward the mark for the prize of the
high calling of God in Christ Jesus.
Philippians 3:14 KJV

love note...

BELOVED, WHEN YOU ARE AFRAID KNOW THAT I AM GOD, YOUR BANNER AND REMEMBER...

*All things work together for good to those
who love and serve Me faithfully...*
Romans 8:28

*The Lord is my light and my salvation;
whom shall I fear?
The Lord is the stronghold of my life;
of whom shall I be afraid?*
Psalm 27:1 ESV

*God is our refuge and strength,
an ever-present help in times of trouble.*
Psalm 46:1 GW

*A thousand may fall at your side,
ten thousand at your right hand,
but it will not come near you.*
Psalm 91:7 NIV

Declaration

by Tosha Jenkins

I promise to love God first, then myself
I promise to trust God
I promise to stop brushing off red flags
      I promise to give God the things that make me feel
         troubled, worried, agitated, or on edge
For the battle is His and He will fight for me
I promise to never allow anyone to take me for granted twice
      I promise to always believe that I matter even
        if someone makes me feel like I don't
      I promise to walk away when my presence and
        absence doesn't hold any value to one
I promise to have no doubt that I deserve the best
I promise to address or question anything that feels like a lie
      I promise to shut down manipulation by a manipulator
        and won't feel guilty for doing so
      I promise to reject, repudiate, or get rid of anything
        or anyone who drains me of energy
I promise to not let anyone disturb my peace
I promise to always spend time in prayer
I promise to believe in God's promises for my life
    I promise to make those tough decisions to align with God's
      obedience even if I don't understand at the moment
I promise to forgive
I promise to accept and heal
    I promise to do what's best for my life and will no longer
      sacrifice my happiness to make others happy
I promise to put God first in everything and anything that I do
I promise to listen to His Instruction and act on it
And have faith that when I do
      God will always make sure I win even when I
        thought I lost all those days
      It wasn't actually loss because God already
        promised that I would gain

THIN LINE BETWEEN LOVE AND HATE

Everyone has a love story to tell. Your first crush. The romantic way your husband proposed. The first time someone said, "I love you." The first taste of Pralines & Cream ice cream. Yes, everyone has a love story to tell.

Nostalgia wraps around your brain like fog at night during one of those horror movies. Yet the moving pictures your brain has conjured up aren't scary at all. They invoke joy and happiness. The good times.

Then, like a freight train at a million miles an hour, the hurt crashes into you, leaving you wondering if you have stepped into the twilight zone. How could the person that brought so much joy, now be the reason for so much pain?

I love you, becomes, I want a divorce.

Revelations leave you feeling sick to your stomach.

Lies and deceit come to light causing you to wonder what you did wrong. How could you have been so blind to it all?

The ice cream goes straight to your thighs.

The hate that you feel courses through your veins like hot lava ready to explode from a once dormant volcano. Bad thoughts, lead to worse decisions just to cope with the pain. We lash out, black out, tune out. We just want out. Out of the pain. Out of the love that led to this pain. We want to do things to help us forget. Things to make them hurt as much as we do.

And just when you think you are done with this person forever, and the hate has filled every living cell of your existence, the realization sets in that the hate is a lie. A. Big. Fat. Lie. You are hurting because you love. You loved with all you had, and it wasn't supposed to end this way. You try to keep a grip on that hate in order to help make this loss easier, but deep down you know the game you are playing only has one winner, and it's not you. Satan is winning and you are handing him the championship trophy.

So now what? Every direction looks dark and bleak. There is no light no matter which way you turn. You might as well be in the middle of an ocean. Those deep dark waters so foreboding, surround you, taunting you to just let go and sink. Your arms are tired from wading in the water.

Yet, there is a small whisper riding the wind. A small voice you hear in your heart. The one that makes you feel a hint of conviction. The one you are crying out to, to help end your agony. He is there. Watching. Waiting for you. Ready to be your comfort rather than turning to your flesh for temporary reprieve, as effective as emptying the Atlantic with a spoon.

He is whispering, "love more." The idea seems foreign and illogical. Why would He ask us to love the person who hurt us, even more? The idea is enough to make you run away or bring you to your knees. You find yourself at a fork in the road. Run or kneel? Your way or God's?

It comes down to a decision. You get to decide. No one, but you. The road of hate. Or the road of love. Only one leads to God's plan for your life. The other, well, just doesn't.

I make it sound so simple. As if one could just flip a switch. As if we had control over who we love, and when we can turn it off. More than anything I wish it were that easy. That we could decide to love so easily, and everything will be instantly well with our lives.
What if you don't want to choose to love? Is it so wrong to protect your heart?

A few hours ago, I stood at the crossroads with a decision to make. I was blindsided by a situation and ended up hurt. I'm not even sure the person that hurt me knows how much or even that they did at all. After battling with my flesh and the hatred that sprung from my heart, I decided to hate. It felt justified. It lasted an hour before I realized how the enemy was pulling my puppet strings.

After seeking God, I ended up choosing love. It wasn't like flipping like a switch. It was difficult. It still is. I chose to love someone, despite the hurt I felt. To let go and let God, do what I can't. I also chose to love myself. I reminded myself that I am beloved, and I give no one the power to make me feel otherwise.

Truth is, love isn't easy. Loving our spouses, significant others, children, family & friends is not always puppies and rainbows. It takes dying to self. It takes loyalty. It takes commitment. It takes always striving to give more and love more, even when you are hurt. It doesn't mean, be a doormat, allow abuse, or unappreciation. It does mean that another person's inability to love you as you love them, doesn't determine who you are and how you love. No one is worth you not living out God's will for your life and who He created you to be.

Not all relationships can come back from the hurt. That's just the reality of life. Couples get divorced. Family's get torn apart. Friendships end. But not all.

Nope, not all! Couples ARE restored! Families ARE reunited. Friendships DO mend. Yet that can only be true for those who choose the path of love. No relationship can mend when we choose to hate. Not one. Not ever.
I began writing this post last night just in a general sense, with just a stirring in my heart. Then today arrived and I woke up to have this road at my feet and had no idea that I would end up teetering on the thin line between love and hate. My life has been so full of peace lately, that this situation that brought me to the crossroads of love and hate, caught me by surprise. Needless to say, it has been a rough day for me, but I am

choosing to love. I am choosing to love others and I am choosing to love myself. I will not allow the enemy to poison my heart with hate. I am a daughter of God and God is love. So most of all, I choose Him.

He directs my steps and will never lead me to anything other than what is good for me, because He chooses love too.

If anyone boasts, "I love God," and goes right on hating his brother or sister, thinking nothing of it, he is a liar. If he won't love the person he can see, how can he love the God he can't see? The command we have from Christ is blunt: Loving God includes loving people. You've got to love both.
1 John 4:19-21 MSG

love note...

BELOVED, WHEN YOU FEEL SHAME, GUILT, OR CONDEMNED, KNOW THAT I AM YOUR REDEEMER ...

I've paid attention to your weeping and stored up all of your tears, not allowing one to go ungathered. I have remembered it all. Beloved, I am on your side, and they can't hurt you.
Psalm 56: 8-9

Blessed [forgiven, refreshed by God's grace] are those who mourn [over their sins and repent], for they will be comforted [when the burden of sin is lifted].
Mathew 5:4 AMPC

PRAYER

Create in me a new, clean heart, O God, filled with clean thoughts and right desires. Don't toss me aside, banished forever from your presence. Don't take your Holy Spirit from me. Restore to me again the joy of your salvation, and make me willing to obey you. Then I will teach your ways to other sinners, and they—guilty like me—will repent and return to you. Don't sentence me to death. O my God, you alone can rescue me.
Psalm 51:10-15 TLB.

Don't Go Ahead of God

A TESTIMONY BY KOREN UTLEY

The Lord himself goes before you and will be with you; he will never leave you nor forsake you. Do not be afraid; do not be discouraged.
Deuteronomy 31:8 NIV

I had everything planned out. After dating for years, I knew this was the man I wanted to spend the rest of my life with. He and I had talked about marriage, and the next thing I knew, a few months later, he invited me to move in with him. I knew moving in before marriage was wrong. A part of me had felt so convicted and uncomfortable living together before marriage, but I loved him and wanted to be with him more than anything. Nevertheless, I battled myself daily.

Initially, I was afraid to tell him of my reservations because I thought he would end the relationship. I didn't want him to think I wasn't ready for commitment. With all my heart I wanted to marry him. However, moving would require me to make some major changes. Resigning from my career of seventeen years and relocating my sons out of state was no small thing. Yet, it not being an easy decision, I still chose love. I chose to make this major move because I believed it was essential for my marital destiny. I won't lie, though. I was terrified.

Growing up in a devout Christian household, and my own personal journey with God, blossomed me into a devoted woman of God. I prayed and fasted about everything in search of guidance and had done so willingly and faithfully for all of my adult life. This time, however, I had had no yearning to pray. In my spirit I already knew the answer. But the heart wanted what it wanted, so I decided to go on a three-day fast in hopes that God would make a way for me to please Him and still have my heart's desire.

One day, after a morning of praise, worship, and prayer, I took a nap, falling into a deep sleep. I dreamt of my car keys in hand, standing outside looking for my car but couldn't find it. A voice nearby snatched my attention and I turned around to it.

"Don't leave before you complete your assignment."

I awoke from the dream and immediately prayed. While in prayer, I heard the voice again.

"Don't leave before you complete your assignment."

There was no doubt in my mind that the Lord was speaking to me.

Yet, I was determined to show God that all would work out. I convinced myself why it would be a good idea to relocate, and finally be with the man I wanted to spend the rest of my life with. I continued the planning process to move, but everything either didn't go smoothly, or began to crumble; including the communication in my relationship with Adam.

One evening my mentor, Apostle Taffy Donzwa, called from London. "Daughter, I have a word for you." I felt sick to my stomach because I knew he had heard from God. He continued, "The Lord said He may change your course, but He will never change His promises. The man that loves and respects you will honor you with marriage. Don't go ahead of God."

God is not man, one given to lies, and not a son of man changing his mind. Does he speak and not do what he

God made you a promise, and He will make good on His word. If you go ahead of God, you will miss the beautiful things that God has purposed and planned for you.

GOD SPOKE. NOW WHAT?

Despite the prophetic warning from a man of God I trusted, I continued the moving process. Desires of the heart can become addictive, and the battle can be difficult to overcome. Letting go of what I wanted for so long would be me breaking my own heart, so I continued planning for what I convinced myself was my blessing. I wasn't about to let the enemy rob me of it either.

I told my parents and tried my best to prepare my sons mentally and emotionally for the move. Everyone was on board because they wanted to see me happy. And although there was general support, which I was grateful for, I knew my mother didn't want me to leave. But I was in love, and I didn't want to take the chance of losing the man I loved.

Within me, the battle raged on. I wanted to be with my future husband but the spirit moving within me refused to be quieted. As a result, I had postponed the moving date several times. Fear of the Lord was the beginning of wisdom, and I was no fool despite my current predicament.

Adam began to apply pressure and asked if I had had a solidified moving date in mind. He had known me well enough and had sensed my fear, yet despite that knowing, he failed to provide me with comfort or assurance that he was my covering, protector, and provider and that moving would be a worthwhile decision. Not a word of support was uttered but I swept that hurt under the rug.

Feeling the pressure and not wanting to lose my opportunity at happiness, I had finally decided I would move at the end of the year and was happy to give Adam the good news. Waiting until the end of the year gave me time to prepare emotionally and spiritually and still show Adam that I was sincere in wanting a full life with him. But just as everything else was not working in my favor, neither had this decision, much to my disappointment.

Adam told me he understood it was a big decision, and if it didn't work out, I could always come back home. My heart dropped and I was speechless. My declaration hadn't been enough. Giving me an escape clause was not what I wanted to hear. I immediately thought, why would anyone be willing to relocate to another state to be with someone that's not willing to reassure you that he would do anything to make it work. I had been willing to give up everything for this relationship. Even go ahead of God. Instead of reassurance that we were in it together, I had been reassured I could return to solitude if it came to that.

A few weeks later, Adam stopped answering my calls and text messages. It was then that I prayed and cried out to God for answers. To my surprise, I didn't hear a word from God.

My God, whom I praise, do not remain silent
Psalm 109: 1 NIV

I felt alone. I had no one to turn to. I was embarrassed because I had convinced my friends, and family that this was a great move for me. After a month of no contact, Adam had finally replied to my text message. He informed me he'd moved on because I showed no signs of following through with moving in with him. My heart was broken. I had never felt pain the way I felt while reading his message. It was a pain I wouldn't wish on anyone. It felt like a death. I grieved for months, crying, and beating myself up for not moving sooner.

Finally, I heard the word of the Lord. Adam had left me, but God hadn't.

> Be careful that you do not forget the covenant of the LORD your God that He made with you; do not make an idol for yourselves in the form of anything He has forbidden you. For the LORD your God is a consuming fire, a jealous God.
> **Deuteronomy 4:23-24 NIV**

God's words increased my tears. I had made an idol out of Adam. Yet I was grateful that I was able to recognize the discipline and conviction of a loving Father and not mistake it for condemnation of a malicious enemy. In my heart I knew God sometimes allowed our hearts to be broken for us to examine where we have made idols out of our relationships. I was willing to go against the will of God for the sake of my relationship. It was then that I realized this was not the plan that God had for my life. His Word is true!

Finally, I heard the word of the Lord. Adam had left me, but God hadn't.

> Be careful that you do not forget the covenant of the LORD your God that He made with you; do not make an idol for yourselves in the form of anything He has forbidden you. For the LORD your God is a consuming fire, a jealous God.
> **Deuteronomy 4:23-24**

God's words increased my tears. I had made Adam out of an idol. Yet I was grateful that I was able to recognize the discipline and conviction of a loving Father and not mistake it for condemnation of a malicious enemy. In my heart I knew God sometimes allowed our hearts to be broken for us to examine where we have made idols out of our relationships. I was willing to go against the will of God for the sake of my relationship. It was then that I realized this was not the plan that God had for my life. His Word is true!

For I know the plans I have for you," declares the LORD, "plans to prosper you and not to harm you, plans to give you hope and a future.
Jeremiah 29:11 NIV

Surely the Sovereign Lord does nothing Surely the Sovereign Lord does nothing without revealing His plan to his servants the prophets.
Amos 3:7 NIV

In retrospect, I remembered it all. God had warned me in spirit. He had sent a prophet to confirm His warning. I could even see it in my mom's apprehension. But I had wanted what I wanted and as a result I tried to go ahead of God. I learned the hard way that when you go ahead of God, nothing will work for you. God's plans are always bigger and better than anything you could imagine.

I FOUND LOVE AGAIN

I was tired of crying and hiding out of embarrassment. The time had come for me to take my life back. I knew God had made me a promise, and all I needed to do was take Him at His Word.

...so is my word that goes out from my mouth: It will not return to me empty, but will accomplish what I desire and achieve the purpose for which I sent it.
Isaiah 55:11 NIV

I started a daily prayer walk. I walked, prayed, and talked to God every day, three times a day for a year. I remember walking for hours with tears in my eyes, heartbroken and wanting to give up, but I was determined to heal and find love again. I spoke words of affirmation and declared the Word of the Lord over my life. I spoke life, love, peace, and joy. I kept speaking life until my tears turned into joy.

They that sow in tears shall reap in joy.
Psalm 126:5 KJV

I felt the peace of God come over me in a way I'd never felt before. I knew it was God. My daily walk turned into a love walk with God. There were days I couldn't wait to go for my love walk. I knew I was going to have a beautiful time with the Lord. My prayers turned into words of gratitude. I couldn't thank God enough for making my heart smile again. Some days I would get in my car and scream with a big smile on face, "Lord, I thank you!" I was so happy. I was growing in love.

One evening after my walk, I fell into a deep sleep. Once again, I dreamt prophetically. I had heard a voice say, "It's time to make a *Bold Move*."

I saw myself in an office helping people discover their purpose and pursue their dreams. It was everything I had prayed for regarding my own purpose. A few weeks later, I launched my coaching business, Bold & Brilliant. I had finally made a bold move. I was soaring high off the success of my business, and love for helping people.

A year later the Lord encouraged me to host a conference. It was nothing new for me to plan a conference but hosting my own was a bold move. I was afraid, as it seemed too soon for such a big undertaking. The timing of God's plan didn't make sense to me. So, I made several attempts to postpone the conference. Seeking guidance, I called my mother and shared my concerns regarding not having enough time.

Mom said, "Daughter, God's timing is perfect. If He tells you to do something, do it. God will give you everything you need to make it happen. Always obey the Lord. Obedience is better than sacrifice."

Months later I hosted my first Bold Life Conference. It was the assignment God told me I needed to complete before leaving. As a result of my obedience, and willingness to follow the Holy Spirit, my life had been transformed as well as the lives of many others. I was finally seeing the light at the end of my heartbreak tunnel, until COVID swept in relentlessly and blew the fuse that had lit me within. I later understood why God kept me from moving ahead; why He kept me where I was. He was giving me a gift I did not know I needed. The gift of quality time before COVID would knock on my door, an unwanted guest, to steal precious life.

Excerpts from the inspirational book
Living the Bold Life
by Self-Development Coach, Koren Utley

love note...

BELOVED, WHEN YOU CAN'T SEE A WAY, KNOW THAT I AM JEHOVAH-JIREH, YOUR PROVIDER...

*Look at the birds! They don't worry about what to eat—
they don't need to sow or reap or store up food—
for your heavenly Father feeds them. And you are
far more valuable to him than they are.*
Matthew 6:26 TLB

*Young lions go hungry and may starve,
but those who seek the Lord's help
have all the good things they need.*
Psalm 34:10 GW

*And God is able to make all grace abound toward you;
that ye, always having all sufficiency in all things,
may abound to every good work*
2 Corinthians 9:8 KJV

*Don't worry about anything; instead,
pray about everything; tell God your needs,
and don't forget to thank him for his answers.*
Philippians 4:6 TLB

HEART OF STONE

Over and over, I have replayed in my head, the words you have spoken and the ones you haven't. The abundance said in anger or perhaps in honesty. The lack of apologies. Each one adding a stony layer over my once fragile heart. I care a little less with each memory of hurt. I withdraw a little more with each tear. My heart was innocent, and faithful, undeserving of all that was heaped upon it. It only did what it was created for. To be loved and give love, but it suffers, nevertheless. It cried out to me for help. For protection.

It took some time, but I've withdrawn so far, I'm floating in the galaxies, beyond the stratosphere of love where only darkness dwells and no living thing can breathe, since crying a river of tears. My once tender heart has hardened like stone, surrounded by an impenetrable shield where it can't be beaten down so easily.

My foolish, naive heart was bold and free, willing to spread its love to anyone, whether deserving of it or not. Compassion and loyalty supposedly its greatest qualities, yet only leading to rejection, abandonment, and pain.

Sometimes, my poor heart cries within the shell of protection, wanting to be bold again. But how can I protect such a tender heart that refuses to listen to reason? That refuses to be cold and unfeeling? I cannot risk hurting again. I never want to hurt like that ever again. I admit, some of the bruises are still healing. Removing my stone shield is not a chance I am ready to take.

Yet, deep inside, I feel a stirring and knowing. It reminds me that not everyone is like you. That not everyone I choose to love will treat me with such indifference. That just because you didn't see my value and appreciate my worth, that everyone else will throw away the traits I have inherited from my Heavenly Father. For isn't He bold and free in giving love, not hiding, despite how wretched humanity can be? No. He chooses to love always. We reject Him. We curse Him. We ignore Him and rebel against Him and yet He continues to love unconditionally.

It has taken some time, but this stirring has grown. With it, some realizations have come to light as scales have fallen from my eyes. In my hurt, I acted out of fear not wisdom and I now know, I wasn't protecting my heart at all. Instead, I was becoming just like you. Indifferent. I cannot let that become who I am.

How I wish you could be a little more caring. How I wish you could be more appreciative. Maybe one day you will be, but I cannot wait until that day. Today, I gladly break my heart free from the self-inflicted bondage I placed it under. It is now free to love others wholeheartedly, including you. That doesn't make me naive or foolish. Not at all. It's just a testament that I am the big-hearted person God created me to be and He doesn't make mistakes. Skillfully & thoughtfully, He made me.

Breaking my hardened heart free from its stone prison doesn't mean I am giving you permission to trample it again. No sir! It means that I am child of God who chooses to walk in her Father's footsteps, and I will unapologetically and proudly be the me, God created me to be.

And I will give you a new heart, and I will put a new spirit in you. I will take out your stony, stubborn heart and give you a tender, responsive heart. And I will put my Spirit in you so that you will follow my decrees and be careful to obey my regulations.
Ezekiel 36:26-27

As**K**oren

Dear Koren,

There is a dirty little secret living within my family. Everyone knows about it, but no one ever speaks about it. During holidays & family gatherings, perpetrators laugh & eat beside their victims wearing the mask of happiness. I find myself wanting to scream it out loud & making my family face it. Expose the perpetrators. But exposing them also exposes their victims. I want to break my family from these chains of bondage. What do I do?

Dear Reader:

Often times, a family secret is masked as protection, but in actuality, it's the total opposite. Family secrets can destroy a family. The only person that's being protected is the perpetrators.

As you said exposing them will also expose their victims. I truly believe this is an issue that needs to be addressed. However, this is a very sensitive issue. I would gently, and compassionately approach the victims to see how they're coping, and if they're ready to deal with this as a family. I would suggest one on one counseling, as well as family counseling. Unresolved family issues are painful and must be handled with love and respect.

Koren,

Bold and Brilliant, Founder
Self-Development Coach

Spiritual Warfare

You had me for years
In fear, stressed, depressed, worried,
and believing in things that didn't
bring nothing but blockage

Now that I'm payin attention,
I'm doin' the blockin'
Stoppin' you and your evil tactics
that have become habit
Im'ma create a tragic situation for you
and bust through
each deceitful temptation and
attack you try to put me through

I pray incessantly
One of the best weapons in this war
Before, after I wake, and in between
I refuse to let you get the best of me
I will not sit around and weep

I fell many times and I got back up to
claim what's mine
My mind has transformed, reformed,
gained, obtained and retained such
wisdom that you can't take away

Eyes open and throwin' defense
to your offense
to make sure we win in the end

We are....
GOD'S
CHILDREN

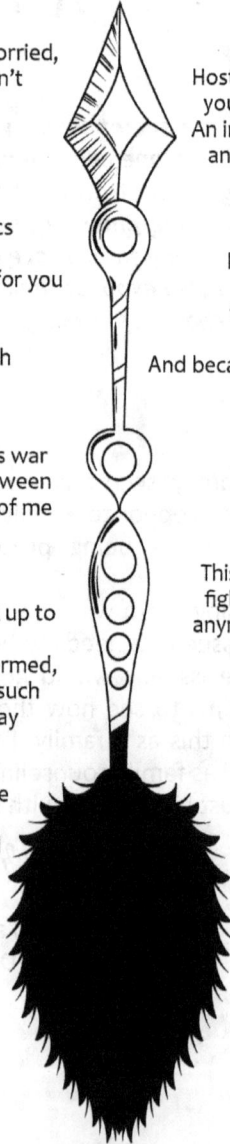

Hostage situations because
you hatin' on my potential
An influential positive force
and it kills you to the core
Now we at war

I'm covered, I have faith,
and I have proven
that I have what it takes
to make it
And because you can't break me
You found the closest
people to me,
to use your evil,
to get at me down

This is deep and I will keep
fightin' until I cannot fight
anymore because you have
declared war on my life

I'm on to you
Those close to me
are on to you

by Tesha Jenkins

love note...

BELOVED, WHEN YOU AT WAR WITHIN, KNOW I AM LAMP UNTO THY FEET AND I WILL GUIDE YOU TO VICTORY...

What causes quarrels and what causes fights among you? Is it not this, that your passions[a] are at war within you? You desire and do not have, so you murder. You covet and cannot obtain, so you fight and quarrel. You do not have, because you do not ask.
James 4:1-2 ESV

There isn't any temptation that you have experienced which is unusual for humans. God, who faithfully keeps his promises, will not allow you to be tempted beyond your power to resist. But when you are tempted, he will also give you the ability to endure the temptation as your way of escape.
1 Corinthians 10:13 GW

Be prepared. You're up against far more than you can handle on your own. Take all the help you can get, every weapon God has issued, so that when it's all over but the shouting you'll still be on your feet. Truth, righteousness, peace, faith, and salvation are more than words. Learn how to apply them... God's Word is an indispensable weapon. In the same way, prayer is essential in this ongoing warfare. Pray hard and long.
Ephesians 6:13-16 MSG

OUT OF THE PIT

It has been my experience that being called to minister encouragement isn't for the faint of heart. I'm sure other ministry leaders can agree. We carry a desire within our hearts to heal the brokenhearted and walking away from a hurting soul is difficult. Like a farmer, planting seeds, that rejoices when he can relish in the fruits of his labor by eating or selling his crop, an encourager rejoices in seeing those souls God placed in our paths, healed, and thriving in life.

Two weeks ago, God painted a picture for me in my prayers. It was of me and a friend of mine, in a pit. I have ministered to this friend for over a year. She has faced her ups and downs. Lately, more downs than ups. In this vision, I am trying as hard as I can to help my friend out of the pit, but she refuses to climb because she is waiting for God to pick her up and bring her out. Every time I feel encouraged and begin to climb the ladder out of the pit, I feel bad for leaving her behind and climb back down into the pit. Again, I try to convince her to take my hand so that I could show her how to climb out, but she shakes her head no, keeping her eyes fixated on the heavens waiting for her miracle.

As I am sitting beside her, I hear God say, "Daughter climb out of the pit."

My heart breaks a little at the idea of leaving my friend. I reply, "I can't leave her down here alone, God."

He says, "You aren't leaving her alone. I am always with her. It is time. You need to walk into your calling, Beloved. She needs to decide if she wants to walk into hers. Child, you have done all you can do. She needs to rise up now."

After that vision, I was both motivated and sad. I cried for my friend because my fear was that she would choose to stay in her pit rather than walk into the calling God placed in her life. The truth is, God calls every one of us to something bigger and greater than ourselves and so many of us miss out on that calling.

I know you are probably wondering, why is it such a bad thing to wait expectantly for God to reach down into the pit and pull you out. It sounds beautiful and heavenly to be miraculously pulled out of a pit. But then what? How have you grown and learned from your trial? You haven't. Now every time you find yourself in a pit, you have only taught yourself to wait for God to provide another miracle. That is not what God is wanting from His people. Climbing out of the pit is part of the journey to grow in Him. To trust in Him. To bring you to the next level of the calling He has placed on your life. It's part of the training and the molding that needs to take place so that God can then use you to help another who has gone through what you have gone through.

My friend was waiting for God to send her help and because He cares, He did. He sent His Word. And He sent me, a friend who could understand & encourage her. He sent her a person that could teach her to climb out and grow in Christ because that friend had traveled that road once before and climbed out of that pit without a miracle.

I shared this vision with my friend, unsure that she would be receptive to it. She replied with tears and then with enthusiasm. I am super excited to report that she has begun her climb out of the pit and allowed me to share this testimony and encouragement with you.

Are you in a pit waiting for a miracle? I would never tell you to stop believing in miracles, but I am going to encourage you to climb out of your pit without relying on one. Use God's Word, and the encouragement of friends to build a ladder and climb out of your pit. You have a calling on your life. The pit was just a pit stop. A necessary part of the journey, but it's not the final destination. Wise up. Rise up. Climb up.

All things are possible for the one who
believes and trusts [in Me]!"
Mark 9:23 AMP

love note...

BELOVED, WHEN YOU ARE TIRED AND CAN'T GO ON, REMEMBER I AM ELOHIM AND YOU ARE MADE IN MY LIKENESS ...

For God did not give us a spirit of timidity (of cowardice, of craven and cringing and fawning fear), but [He has given us a spirit] of power and of love and of calm and well-balanced mind and discipline and self-control.
2 Timothy 1:7 AMPC

You can make many plans, but the Lord's purpose will prevail.
Proverbs 19:21 NLT

"If I make you light-bearers, you don't think I'm going to hide you under a bucket, do you? I'm putting you on a light stand. Now that I've put you there on a hilltop, on a light stand—shine! Keep open house; be generous with your lives. By opening up to others, you'll prompt people to open up with God, this generous Father in heaven.
Matthew 5:14-16 MSG

My grace is sufficient for thee: for my strength is made perfect in weakness.
2 Corinthians 12:9

Exhale

My diagnosis is zeal for God
The prognosis could be that
of many forms that
RESTORE

CURE

ALLEVIATE

What did it take to finally surrender?
What did it take to make me fall to my knees
and scream His name?

HYPERVENTILATING
feeling like I'm heading to life support
And in the next moment, I'm *reborn*
Bouncing back from the bottom
and registering the experience as a resistance

Old ways nonexistent because new behaviors are extremely relevant to
the present that paves the way to my future
Principalities no longer have me in a back and forth sham reality
The prime target was to distract and kill my faith and make me walk the
plank of death
To make me believe I had nothing left

But God had a different plan
My life is in His hands no matter what he said, he did,
no matter what she said, or what she did
My will is to live
My will is to

OBTAIN
RETAIN
MAINTAIN
and SUSTAIN
the faith that dwells in Jesus's name

No weapon formed against me shall prosper
What was dark now is light
What died now lives
Where there was pain, has now been replaced with peace

God will never forsake me
no matter what the enemy wants me to believe
The process of greatness, makes this all the more necessary even when we
don't understand God's plan in that time
When you fall in line and align, you will be blessed with clarity
No more wondering

You too paid a price
Sacrificed what was for what is now
Humbly stand proud and allow God's light
that lives within to shine loud
It will speak volumes to every battle that assumed it would destroy you

You took it all in
You prayed
You fought
You prayed
You won

And you prayed with praise

You didn't fail

You've earned this moment

To rejoice

To

exhale

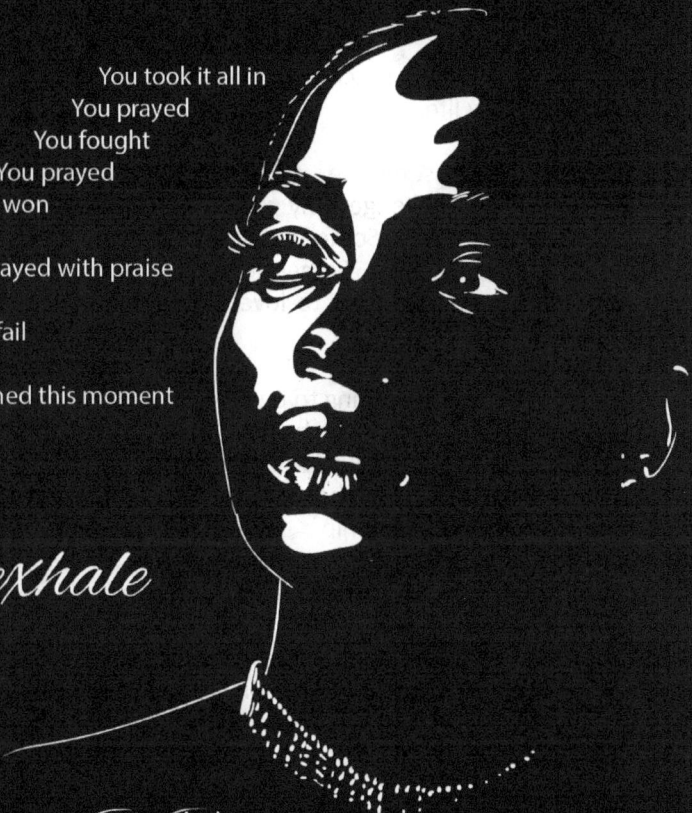

by Tosha Jenkins

GROWING OR DYING

Several days ago, I sat in a chair waiting to be called back into an important meeting that had the potential to change my life. I should have been nervous or perhaps even excited, but as it were, I was neither. I sat there and eyed a plant on the small table beside me. One large leaf had begun to decay & wither. I couldn't help but stare at it. I was transfixed by this one leaf showing signs of both life and death. At its root, its color was deep green and shiny. At its end, it was browned and dry, beginning to crumble.

I was in awe at how much that one leaf seemed to resemble a situation in my life.

You see, I met someone. An absolutely amazing someone. Someone who challenged my mind. Someone that challenged me to try love again. Someone who challenged me to see the world with new eyes. Someone who challenged me to be vulnerable again. Not just to love but to life. A very beautiful someone.

As I sat in that chair waiting to be called back into a meeting that could change my life for the better, I could only stare at this leaf and think about that beautiful someone who made a decision on behalf of us both. That beautiful someone wanted to take a break from our relationship.

As I stared & waited, I reflected on the conversations we shared and the decisions that I believe led to that fateful decision. In fact, I had contemplated the same thing once before myself. Staring at the leaf I surmised that in life and relationships, we are either growing or dying. There is no in between. The things we do and say either bring life or death to our lives and relationships.

Choosing to do nothing and say nothing doesn't change that. Doing and saying nothing is most emphatically still bringing growth or death to a situation or relationship.

Pondering the leaf, I wondered what decision or lack thereof, its caretaker made that affected its life. A decision that this poor plant had no control over. Was the caretaker too busy to water and nurture the plant as it needed? Was she ignorant of what the plant needed to survive?

That same caretaker caught me off guard when she interrupted my thoughts with a question. "Do you know anything about plants?" She pointed to the plant that arrested my attention. "I don't know how to keep it alive. I just watered it yesterday. It's a large pot of mixed plants. Perhaps I should repot them in individual pots."

I smiled at her many suggestions before I placed a finger to the soil. "It needs to be watered again," I advised her feeling its dryness. She seemed surprised at my suggestion and reiterated her having already taken that course of action. I repeated my advice. It occurred to me that she was not negligent but perhaps shouldn't own this particular plant as she did not know what it needed.

The thought brought me to my emotional knees. My beautiful someone's words echoed in my head. "Just because you want to be "the one" for someone else, doesn't mean you are. Just because you may know how to be good to someone doesn't mean you are necessarily good for someone in particular. Your good, may not be the good they particularly need."

So many emotions flooded me. I looked at this woman and wanted to snatch the plant and run. Not because she was neglectful. She seemed to truly care about doing good for this plant. The problem was, this woman's good was still bringing death to her plant. Her good, was not the right good. Her wanting the plant to live was simply not enough.

I couldn't help but wonder if this break in my relationship was to bring life or death to it. Perhaps I am not "the good" my beautiful one needs, despite me being a genuinely good person. It hurts to admit that to myself. No one wants to believe themselves deficient. While that may most certainly be the case, I had to change my perspective. It's not about my perceived deficiency. It's about growing or dying.

Do I want to, every so often, water my cute plant, but still watch it die? No. That would be selfish. Do I want to BE the plant that is dying? Of course not. No one does. We all want a caretaker who is going to address our needs in a way that promotes growth & life. We should all want to be the caretaker that offers the same.

I had to see my relationship like that plant's relationship with its caretaker and respect that the plant just wants to be loved & nurtured properly in order to grow & not die. We are all, both the plant & caretaker. We all want to be loved well, & love others well. I had to understand that this beautiful person I met needed me to understand that.

Do I care what the end result is? Of course, I do. But I also care that it's the best result for us both & not one that will lead to wasted time & regrets.

You see, I get to choose growth or death for my heart and well being. Not being the right person for someone doesn't make me less valuable or worthy of love. Not at all. I am choosing to be better for myself, not bitter, no matter the outcome of the break.

I am choosing to trust God to be the gardener that will prune away hurt, selfishness, pride & immaturity. I am trusting Him to plant me in good soil, water me, nurture me, and shine His Son's light on me. I am trusting Him for my growth so that I will be the right good for someone, who in turn is the right good for me.

"Words kill, words give life; they're either poison or fruit—you choose."
Proverbs 18:21 MSG

And the seeds that fell on the good soil represent honest, good-hearted people who hear God's word, cling to it, and patiently produce a huge harvest.
Luke 8:15 NLT

love note...

BELOVED, I AM EL ROI, THE ONE WHO SEES YOU. WHEN YOU FEEL LOST, REJECTED AND LONELY, REMEMBER MY PROMISES...

"...for He has said, "I will never [under any circumstances] desert you [nor give you up nor leave you without support, nor will I in any degree leave you helpless], nor will I forsake or let you down or relax My hold on you [assuredly not]!"
Hebrews 13:5 AMP

"For the eyes of the Lord roam throughout the earth, so that He may strongly support those whose heart is completely His."
2 Chronicles 16:9 NASB

"And I will ask the Father, and he will give you another advocate to help you and be with you forever ... I will not leave you as orphans [comfortless, bereaved, and helpless]; I will come [back] to you.
John 14:16-18 AMP

The Night I Said Yes

A TESTIMONY BY TOSHA JENKINS

The moonlight bounced off the water from the in-ground pool onto my best friend's new home. I had been eager to get out of Camden for a for few days and when she asked if I wanted to the spend the weekend at her house, I jumped at the chance. After dinner, I made my way over to a chair lounge to get comfortable. It was the perfect place to roll my weed. Kids weren't around. The dark was peaceful and quiet. The stars littered the sky. The scenery alone had me in a calm state, but my weed would elevate me to euphoria.

I closed my eyes, laid back and sparked up my dutch, star-gazing. I longed to be as high as those stars. As I puffed away, my thoughts circled back to where they always had and probably why I needed my high daily. Where do I go from here? I had been writing poetry and performing spoken word for years. I had done shows and had sparks of reaching higher levels of success only to be doused by this or that. I knew I was meant to have more. Be bigger. Midway into my dutch, an unexplainable feeling came over me. I'd been smoking for thirty years and it most definitely wasn't the weed. I sat up feeling weird.

I heard a voice say, "Put it out. You're done."

At that moment, I wondered if maybe it had been the weed. I'd never been so high that I'd heard voices. I had only taken a few puffs. I looked around to see if anyone had been around, but I was alone. I sat silent for a moment before the feeling got stronger. I looked up to the sky as I leaned to my left and proceeded to brush the dutch against the ground until it went out. I stood up and threw it into the darkness behind me and

55

didn't look back. My thoughts were screaming and scrambling in my mind. *What's happening? What's going on?* I was in such shock that I stood speechless for a few minutes trying to process what just happened.

I wanted to run but my legs would not heed my request. I walked toward the house and looked up again freaked out. I heard that same voice ask, "Are you ready?"

I don't know why but I answered, "Yes." When I got inside the house, I walked over to my best friend who was sitting in front of her fireplace engrossed in her thoughts.

She looked at me and could tell I was startled. "What's wrong? You look like you saw a ghost."

I explained what happened and it was as if she knew. She wasn't spooked. My best friend is a woman of God and I have witnessed God work through her. I've also witnessed God bless her in ways that left my stupefied.

August 15, 2020 was the night God spoke to me. He touched me in such a way I emptied my purse and pockets leaving all of my stash and paraphernalia with my best friend. I did not want it. Any of it. She promised to discard it. It's been over two years since I ended my smoking addiction. Cold turkey. I smoked on and off for over thirty years and in just one word from God it was no longer a part of my life. I don't miss it or crave it. At all.

From there, other addictions began to fall from me. I had been an avid follower and believer in Astrology and Numerology. Daily I would receive a handful of astrology readings from different websites, telling me my future, mood and anything else that I found fascinating and viable. Numbers plagued me and I was addicted to researching angel numbers. Until one day, my best friend and I were discussing it and she told me what the Bible said about astrology and such. I nearly cried. For so long I had been hanging my hopes on believing that my astrology and fortune telling would come to pass. I began to doubt the validity but needed a hope to hang on to. But my relationship with God had begun to deepen and the need to hang onto anything he disproved of quickly made me turn a new leaf. I deleted hundreds of daily horoscope emails and unsubscribed from all of them. I was done. Just like that. I had even stopped drinking alcohol daily, drinking wine occasionally.

In the place those addictions left me empty, God filled me up. Rather than reading horoscopes daily, I read my bible and journaled. Prayer filled my atmosphere instead of the marijuana smoke. Genuine joy rather than effects of drunkenness caused me to dance and leap like I had no sense.

I am beyond grateful. Only God is responsible for my cleanliness.

Wash me clean from my guilt. Purify me from my sin. For I recognize my rebellion; it haunts me day and night. Against you, and you alone, have I sinned; I have done what is evil in your sight. You will be proved right in what you say, and your judgment against me is just. For I was born a sinner— yes, from the moment my mother conceived me. But you desire honesty from the womb, teaching me wisdom even there. Purify me from my sins, and I will be clean; wash me, and I will be whiter than snow. Oh, give me back my joy again; you have broken me— now let me rejoice.
Psalm 51:2-8 NLT

FROM DEATH TO LIFE

Today has been a day of death. Two relationships have officially ended. It was also officially my last day of work at a place I loved. All three deaths were painful to my heart. Two of these deaths I initiated, one I had to accept. Nevertheless, I find my sacrifices crucifying my heart to a cross.

Today is my "Good Friday."

It seems strange to refer to so much pain as good. Let me assure you, it is far from good. I'm immensely sad. My heart is bleeding. I want the sorrow to end.

Yet, it is a sorrow I need to endure. Just as Jesus chose to sacrifice His life and die for our salvation, sometimes in life, we must also choose to kill off what is not producing the life God wants us to have.

It's never easy. It hurts. But it's necessary.

I won't give details regarding the relationships that have ended because I respect the privacy of others. I will say that sometimes people are only in your life for a reason and a season. And when those reasons and seasons have passed, we must learn to not hold on to what doesn't belong in the next chapters of our lives. Whether it was their choice or yours to end the relationship, we have to be just as willing to let go of them as we are willing to break those ties.

We must also understand that death isn't the end. The burial of a seed is the beginning of a new harvest. If we only focused on the seed being buried, we can never appreciate the harvest it produces and how it blesses our lives.

Jesus resurrected after His Good Friday. The ENTIRE purpose of His Good Friday was for His resurrection. It was necessary to bring forth the victory God had planned all along.

If the Lord permits me to see Monday, it will be part of my "Resurrection Sunday." You see, I had to leave a job I love because an amazing new opportunity came into my life and I begin a new job on Monday. One that will benefit my life, children & future. Not only is this new job a wonderful opportunity in and of itself, but it also has the potential to help kick start a dream that I never thought would come to fruition.

I don't know what will come of my ended relationships, but I do trust that God will never let it be a meaningless loss. Something good will come from the sacrifice of letting go.

You see, God will never have us sacrifice for nothing. He is a loving and giving God. What He puts to death is to bring forth a better life, calling, future, character, ministry, relationship, career, Kingdom. Our "Good Fridays" are never in vain and if we just wait a little while, we can fully expect our "Resurrection Sundays" and all the rejoicing that comes with the victory.

For the Lord will not abandon him forever. Although God gives him grief, yet he will show compassion too, according to the greatness of his loving-kindness. For he does not enjoy afflicting men and causing sorrow.

My eyes flow day and night with never-ending streams of tears because of the destruction of my people. Oh, that the Lord might look down from heaven and respond to my cry! My heat is breaking over what is happening to the young girls of Jerusalem.

But I called upon your name, O Lord, from deep within the well, and you heard me! You listened to my pleading; you heard my weeping! Yes, you came at my despairing cry and told me not to fear.

O Lord, you are my lawyer! Plead my case!
For you have redeemed my life.
Lamentations 3: 31-58 TLB

5 Years Later

I can hardly believe it's already been five years since I wrote From Death To Life. Back then there was no way of telling exactly what would happen after experiencing those "deaths." So many times, we want to hold on to people, places and things because we love them. Not that that is a bad thing, but the heart can often be deceitful and doesn't know what is best for us.

As a child of God, I had to simply trust Him to guide me once I laid my burdens at His feet. I had to fight myself from rushing back to His feet and snatching back all I had left there. But I didn't because His will and plans are always perfect. I had to trust Him more than I trusted myself. The thing about trusting God is, sometimes He goes far above and beyond what we dared hope.

The two relationships I mentioned in my original letter, were never restored. While that may seem sad, in retrospect, God was protecting me from people who would keep me from my purpose, and who had taken and taken and taken some more, depleting me. God cut off the proverbial leaches to save me from being sucked dry.

I learned that I am a giver and oftentimes give too much of myself or allow others to take without restraint. God has taught me to create boundaries and give with a Good Samaritan Spirit. He helped the poor on the road and set him up with help but did not take the poor man home. He helped and gave within boundaries.

While God dried up that stream, He opened another gushing with love, success and joy. My new job had proved to be a blessing, I could have never expected. Not only did my income increase significantly, I met my now best friend (and co-author).

Only God can orchestrate such a situation. We literally sat next to each other at work. One day she began to talk of the projects she was working on. She was a writer and a poet. She had a blog and worked at a radio station. I was silently impressed. She was a bit intimidating, so I kept quiet.

One day she showed me a logo design someone had created for her and said she wasn't entirely sure she liked it. She was trademarking her logo and was getting merchandise printed. I don't know why I did, but I offered to create a design for her. She looked at me as if I had had ten heads. I hadn't told her that I did a little graphic design.

She agreed and the following day I presented her with a few options. Upon seeing them, her eyes opened wide and I could see how much she loved my designs. She chose her favorite and trademarked the design I had created.

Shortly after, she mentioned a multi-author book project she had been asked to be part of. It piqued my interest and I asked for more details. I had written in a long time and had had no desire to do so. But something about this project moved me and I found myself asking her if she could talk to the publisher on my behalf so I too could submit a short story. She did and I was approved to submit my story. Both of our stories were published and since then we have been inseparable.

My passion to write returned with full force. Since then, I have founded Urban House Publishing and have published a dozen of my own books, plus other authors, including Tosha. She and I have collaborated on some many projects. While all of those accomplishments are wonderful, the most amazing success was Tosha giving her life to the Lord and living for God with a blazing passion after seeing God's light through me. Her words, not mine.

God may have ended two relationships and a good job, but He gave me a better job and a friendship that is worth more to me than both the previous relationships combined.

God will never take from you, to not give you better. Never. We just have to learn to let go and trust He will place better in our hands.

See, I am doing a new thing!
Now it springs up; do you not perceive it?
I am making a way in the wilderness and streams
in the wasteland. The wild animals honor me, the
jackals and the owls, because I provide water in the
wilderness and streams in the wasteland, to give
drink to my people, my chosen
Isaiah 43:19-20 NIV

AsKoren

Dear Koren,

I'm a single and newly born-again woman. I am actively dating someone who isn't necessarily saved, although he does believe in God & Jesus. I am feeling convicted about sex before marriage but because we're already sexually active, telling him that I want to save myself for marriage may seem like I'm pressuring him for a commitment, which I am not. I know I am not yet ready to be a wife. How do I approach him about me wanting to live right & not make him feel like I'm using abstinence as a bargaining chip?

Dear Reader:

I want to encourage you to never feel guilty for deciding what you feel is best for you. You have a right to change your mind. Hard conversations are hard but necessary. I always suggest to couples, that if you want someone to hear you, always approach them with love and respect. Be honest, open, and clear about what you want. If you're feeling convicted about sex before marriage, have the talk. The way you start isn't always the way you have to end with a person. Over time, your values, and desires tend to change. If at some point in your life you realize what you were doing no longer serves you or makes you happy, you have the right to make the necessary changes.

Koren,

Bold and Brilliant, Founder
Self-Development Coach

THIS IS ME

For Christmas my church produced a play inspired by the movie, The Greatest Showman with a Christian twist - The Greatest Story Ever Told. The children's cast did an amazing job portraying circus acts that reflect the biblical accounts. The three Hebrew Boys were fire jumpers. Daniel was a Lion Tamer. And a few other relatable stories.

Afterward, I was able to watch the actual movie for the first time and it truly resonated with me. (If you haven't watched the movie, you should.) I'm not a bearded lady or a contortionist but I know what it feels like to be talked down to and made to feel bad about yourself. I know what rejection feels like all too well. Everyone in life has been rejected at one time or another, but to be rejected on levels that wounds so deeply you feel your heart shatter is another matter entirely, especially when it comes at the hand of someone you care about.

There are many scenes throughout the movie of rejection. The entire movie is based on being rejected in all walks and stages of life. In all areas of life. But there is one particular scene that made me love the movie. The "This Is Me" number. You'll just have to watch it to see why.

Life is filled with rejection. Not everyone is going to love you. But not everyone is going to reject you either. In fact, finding the chosen few who are for you is a blessing. Jesus preached to the multitudes, but His circle were only a chosen few. And because that's life, one of the chosen few betrayed him. But that didn't stop His purpose. In fact, it propelled it.

God fearfully and wonderfully made us. He knit us together in the way He wanted us to be. He doesn't make mistakes. He fashioned us in the way we are for a purpose. I have learned to accept and appreciate that I am not a 5'10 long-legged beauty. I accept that I shouldn't grace any athletic facility as anything other than a spectator. I accept that I am no rocket scientist. I accept that I'm not winning any housekeeping or cooking awards. I am simply me. A mom, that works full time, loves to write, and is a nerd. This is me. And God will place those who will appreciate me for me, in my path. I trust Him for it. He has already begun to do so.

I urge you to watch the movie and listen to This Is Me. It's become my anthem of sorts. And remember that you are worth every bit of love you crave. You are glorious.

> *We demolish arguments and every pretension that*
> *sets itself up against the knowledge of God, and*
> *we take captive every thought to make it*
> *obedient to Christ.*
> **2 Corinthians 10:5 NIV**

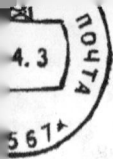

Signed, Sealed & Delivered

You are not being denied
You are being prepared
God is bigger than any problem,
any struggle, and any hurt
So don't put limits on Him
He knows what you need and when you need it
Perfect Timing

He is your shelter when you have no one to turn to
An open line of communication
to utilize when things are taking a toll
And when things are going right in life
He is the Potter and will mold you into His masterpiece
To send you on a path of unfamiliar territory
Protection and guidance included on a secluded mission
His love for you knows no bounds

The sound of His voice can be found in His Word
Study Him
Spend time with Him
Embrace Him
Love Him
Because He loves you
A reciprocal relationship that will change you and your life

Will you heed the call?
Will you trust Him?
Will you love Him?
Will you allow Him to love you without interference?
Can you hear it?
You're being called

Allow God to work through your brokenness
Trust Him to make you whole
No one will be able to hold you down
when God is about to elevate you
There was a contract
There was a promise before you were born
It's already been signed for approval
It is time to claim what's yours

by Tosha Jenkins

SPEND MY LIFE

I'm not a person who particularly ever enjoyed shopping, although now that I've lost a significant amount of weight, it's a much more tolerable experience. I've just never been much of a spender. Money doesn't burn a hole in my pocket so to speak. I would say my attitude toward spending is healthy and balanced. Sometimes I spend because I need and other times because I want.

Today, I actually went out and bought myself a ton of clothes. A very rare occurrence for me. It was more out of necessity than desire. As I mentioned before, I've lost a lot of weight, which has forced me to buy a completely new wardrobe.

After looking at all my purchases, I was content that I filled a need & wouldn't have to stress about what to wear to work. I was more satisfied with solving a problem then having cute news clothes, although I did get some really cute items. I began thinking about how we go through life seeking to spend to get things (a new car, house, clothes, technology, etc) and yet, most of us think little as to how we spend our lives.

Our time, our hearts, our words are often mismanaged. We treat them as if we have an endless supply of fresh days in which to make meaningful choices regarding each.

Words are spoken without thought. Time is spent without purpose. People treat relationships like tissue, using & discarding.

I realized with such clarity that I don't want to waste another minute frivolously spending my life. I only have one life to live and I want to make each moment count. How I spend my life is more important to me, than how I spend money.

My time. My heart. My words. They are more valuable than stocks, bonds, gold, diamonds, cash. I want to be mindful of where I invest my most precious commodities.

I want to forgive quickly & not waste time in anger or bitterness when I can spend it in love & making new and lasting memories.

I want to find a purpose and make a positive difference in the lives of others.

I want to build up others, encouraging them to be more, see more, do more, love more.

I want to spend my life with those actively enriching my life. In turn, I want to actively enrich theirs.

I have a friend that expressed concern about the legacy being left to his children. Now I see, nothing is more meaningful than how we choose to spend our lives with them, not on them. Yes, they love video games, clothes, and toys but what they will come to cherish are the memories and how we molded their lives. The same applies to our significant others & friends.

How we choose to spend our lives and with whom, is an investment. Do so wisely.

But now put these things out of your life: anger, bad temper, doing or saying things to hurt others, and using evil words when you talk. Do not lie to each other... So always do these things:

Show mercy to others; be kind, humble, gentle, and patient. Do not be angry with each other, but forgive each other. If someone does wrong to you, then forgive him. Forgive each other because the Lord forgave you.

Do all these things; but most important, love each other. Love is what holds you all together in perfect unity. Let the peace that Christ gives control your thinking...

Use all wisdom to teach and strengthen each other.
Colossians 5 ICB

love note...

BELOVED, I AM JEHOVAH RAPHA, THE ONE WHO HEALS, AND WHENEVER YOU FEEL UNWELL IN MIND, HEART, OR BODY REMEMBER MY PROMISES ...

I'll come with healing, curing the incurable
Jeremiah 30:17 MSG

I will take away sickness from among you
Exodus 23:25 NIV

I will bring it health and cure, and I will cure them, and will reveal unto them the abundance of peace and truth.
Jeremiah 33:6 KJV

Dear friend, listen well to my words; tune your ears to my voice. Keep my message in plain view at all times. Concentrate! Learn it by heart! Those who discover these words live, really live; body and soul, they're bursting with health.
Proverbs 4:20-22 MSG

Dear Beloved Bride,

Bind yourself to me and allow me to lead you in love, not in domination. Lower your walls and trust me to cover you in your vulnerability.

As your heavenly Husband, I will care for you unselfishly. It is my duty to make you feel beautiful and loved. To inspire you to blossom and I will do so wholeheartedly in every way possible.

And when the time comes that I join you to an earthly husband, you will never settle for less than how I have loved you.

Jesus, Your Boo

Inspired by Ephesians 5:22-28

LEAVE A REVIEW

Would you consider leaving a review after reading? We read each one and appreciate the support and feedback!

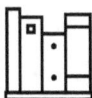

OTHER BOOKS YOU MAY ENJOY

About The Author

Cynthia Marcano is Wall Street Journal Best-selling author, enamored of Jesus, reading, and cake. Born and raised in Southern New Jersey to Puerto Rican parents, she loves to incorporate her roots and culture as a Christian and Hispanic woman into her fiction writing.

She founded Feeding Thousands Publishing, a company devoted to Her Christian works, in 2015 and now having over ten books published encompassing her own works and the works of others.

In 2019 she founded Urban House Publishing. A platform used to help aspiring writers of color develop their talents and release media breaking the stereotypical they are usually portrayed as in books and film. Soon after, Cynthia won Best Short Story for local newspaper in Camden County, New Jersey, her first achievement in writing.

She Will Rise, a brand devoted to encouraging others through heartbreak and loss was also launched in 2019 to empower women into business, inner and outer beauty, and self-care. Through her organization, Cynthia leads women on encouragement "journeys" of self-discovery and self-love.

In 2022, Cynthia, along with a host of other successful writers achieved Wall Street Journal Bestseller success for title Writer's Success Secrets, it reaching #4 on the list.

Cynthia is a loving mother to three beautiful children and now resides in Dallas, TX.

www.CynthiaMarcano.com
Facebook - @AuthorCynthiaMarcano
Instagram -@Urban_House_Publishing

About The Author

Tosha D. Jenkins also known as Indian Spice is a native of Camden, New Jersey. Being an accomplished writer in all forms; a poet, author, ghost writer, song writer, and a spoken word artist. Tosha uses her gift to encourage, inspire, and uplift.

Her writing transitioned to the level of author, in 2010, when she self-published her first two novels. That same year, she was recognized by the mayor of Camden City, New Jersey and received an award for achievements.

Throughout the years, Tosha has performed and opened for many shows as a spoken word artist. Her passion to perform and share her gift and talent has touched many people during her journey in writing.

With a compassion for the brokenhearted, Tosha founded and established the brand, Broken Hearts Still Beat (BHSB) in 2018.

In 2019, Tosha became the first published author at Urban House Publishing where two more books have been published. Under the tutelage of Cynthia Marcano, Founder and CEO of Urban House Publishing, Tosha has elevated her natural talents to write as not just a poem but as a Psalmist while also laying the foundations to master screenwriting.

In 2023, Jesus My Boo, became her first publication under the title of Psalmist, a purpose she has embraced emphatically and proudly to help minister, encourage, and inspire many women across the globe.

About The Author

About The Author

A native of Illinois, Koren Utley is a mother, Minister, and Certified Self-Development Coach. At a young age, Koren knew she wanted to make a difference in the world. Koren was raised in a Christian home and started working in ministry at a young age. At the age of 10 years old, Koren asked God who am I and why am I here? The curiosity about life and her purpose on earth started early. Koren always asked questions and anything she did not understand, she would thoroughly research until she found the answers. Koren learned early on, that life is about living the questions and discovering the answers. Koren always knew she was called to impact but had no idea how to get started or when to start. Koren knew God had plans for her life, but there was so much more she knew she needed to learn.

Koren continued her journey by attending leadership trainings, workshops, and professional life coach training. Koren was also trained as an Elder and completed a 12-month Discipleship program.

Koren has dedicated her life to helping others. In 2003, she started a mentoring program dedicated to helping young adults develop coping strategies and build their emotional resilience. Koren has always been passionate about helping people from all walks of life. In 2007, Koren extended her Life coaching program Internationally. Koren has worked with clients in Uganda, Botswana, Europe, and Zimbabwe. For the last 15 years, Koren has worked with local churches, and corporations, building strategy teams, focused on leadership training.

In 2014, Koren completed a local and international school of the prophet's program under the leadership of Prophet Elijah Kalayagosi, and in 2018 Prophet Aldi Essandjo.

Koren is the founder of Bold and Brilliant, founded in 2017, an organization developed to equip and empower men and women from all walks of life to discover their God-given purpose and live their dreams. Koren is also the founder of Dinner at the Table, an organization focused on bringing families back to the table and putting an end to hunger. Dinner at the table goes beyond the meal.

Of all her accomplishments, Koren is most proud of the Life she has built with her three sons. It has been an incredible journey of living a life that is full, and impactful.